SOAR TO SUCCESS

SOAR TO SUCCESS

IVY BLAIR

CONTENTS

1. Introduction — 1
2. Section 1: Understanding Success and Inner Harmony — 5
3. Section 2: Cultivating a Growth Mindset — 9
4. Section 3: Setting Meaningful Goals — 13
5. Section 4: Time Management and Productivity — 17
6. Section 5: Building Resilience and Overcoming Chal — 21
7. Section 6: Nurturing Inner Harmony — 25
8. Section 7: Cultivating Positive Relationships — 29
9. Section 8: Embracing Change and Adaptability — 33
10. Conclusion — 37

Copyright © 2024 by Ivy Blair
All rights reserved. No part of this book may be reproduced in any manner whatsoever without written permission except in the case of brief quotations embodied in critical articles and reviews.
First Printing, 2024

CHAPTER 1

Introduction

Are you seeking actionable insights to soar to success in life? Do you wish to shine like a rock star in both your personal and professional lives? If you answered yes, congratulations! You have arrived at the ultimate guide to exercises and practical wisdom for leading a purpose-fueled, harmonious, and successful life. Success coaches have identified time-tested and proven strategies to enhance ventures for many individuals, and these strategies can work for you as well!

Leading a truly joyful life—that's the goal. Our secret list delves into various methods for becoming cheerful, successful, and forthcoming. Before we embark on our journey, we must learn the fundamental tunes of society. Sustaining a persistent objective to be content is more than just an excellent goal; it's a resolution that stands the test of time. Healthy, stress-free living leads to long-term happiness—a balanced blend of existence, work, financial needs, family requirements, and personal joy.

By giving people something to hope for and setting realistic targets, we assist in achieving fulfillment. We learn how to stop worrying about meeting others' expectations and focus on our desires. Smiling and laughing are essential to this journey. Remember, "beneath an unsatisfied human, a wonderful human is hiding." This book will guide you in uncovering that wonderful human within.

Purpose of the Book

The primary aim of this book is to blend the motivation to soar with the knowledge and strategies on how to achieve it. It is designed to inspire, inform, and induct you into the realm of possibilities rather than merely preparing you for probabilities in our competitive world. Furthermore, the book emphasizes the importance of purpose and inner harmony as the cornerstones of a balanced journey to success.

This book serves four main purposes:

- **To elevate the vision of readers** by focusing on their purpose, mission, and innovation.
- **To uplift the state of their body, mind, and spirit.**
- **To enable excellence** in all aspects of their lives, including personal, professional, community, home, and duties.
- **To celebrate their indomitable power** to express themselves in all possible ways.

The approach in this text is to simplify the process of balancing one's life at an intellectual level, breaking down complex subjects into simple, understandable, and easily accessible language. The purpose of this book is to orient your mind to broaden your vision and thinking process to solve problems and achieve your objectives.

The basic objectives of this book are to enable you to:

- Develop managerial abilities and skills.
- Acquire the qualities of successful managers and outstanding leadership, commitment, and dedication.
- Become a better communicator.

- Lead, motivate, build, and manage an effective team.
- Master tactics and techniques for managing, controlling, co-ordinating, and supervising activities.
- Gain insight into the latest information technology.
- Make informed decisions in any given situation.

CHAPTER 2

Section 1: Understanding Success and Inner Harmony

What does it mean to be successful in your life? This question spans across all areas of life, from business to teaching to home life. According to Richard Carlson, Ph.D., "The best way to obtain success in your life is to follow the advice that your inner nature gives you, cherish it, and value it." While this may seem easier said than done, there are practices that can help us get there. Success is no more or less than your internal and external experience of life. We might view others as successful, but it doesn't mean that they perceive themselves as such. Everyone can achieve success.

In **Soar to Success: Practices for Purpose and Inner Harmony**, the author Ivy Blair maps out the possibilities of lasting success, true to the nature of humanity and life. In the end, it is not even success that we pursue, but rather purpose and inner harmony.

We encourage you to explore with us the elements of what it takes to live a life that is both successful and deeply satisfying, whatever your definition of success may be. How can you live up to this definition of success? Learn the age-old practices that can reduce anxiety, stress, and other negative effects of modern life. As Sri Chinmoy eloquently stated, "The words I like come from cooking, to test for inner harmony. When the food is harmonious, it's successful." The practice of following your truth, your inner harmony, and inner principles is simple but not easy. The payoffs for life's successes and happiness are immense. Join us in the practices outlined in this book.

Defining Success

One fundamental definition of "success" that I teach to MBA students is: "Obtaining that which is desired or intended." This definition helps leaders, and future business leaders understand that elements or factors of success reside within us and are also manifest in our creations and relationships. Success is a wise pursuit; we do not seek that which we do not value. Similarly, when we achieve our goals, a tremendous sense of accomplishment follows. The more we believe that our goals are truly aligned with who we are, what we value, and what we wish to express, the more joy and fulfillment we experience.

As a good business leader or a whole person, you are a "possibilist." This does not mean indulging in "fantasy" thinking or declaring that you are special a priori. Rather, it signifies understanding that possibilities and opportunities exist within environments and possessing the skill to sniff them out. It also means recognizing that not all possibilities are worthy of investment, and that failure presents its own gifts.

Only you can decide what you want to accomplish. To conduct a meaningful examination of what is important amid the brambles of life, I perform a "to life-plan" exercise with many of my clients. The "to-do" list is rarely the hard part. The tough part involves determining the intentions and values that give direction to the mundane tasks and duties. Perform this "to life-plan" when making one of those critical life choices.

Exploring Inner Harmony

Although inner harmony may not be valued as highly in the external world as talents and competences, can we deny that its absence is conspicuous? We cannot ignore disharmony without suffering adverse effects. We must acknowledge both disharmony and inner harmony. Inner harmony is as much about tending and practicing the self as it is about abilities. We can achieve it when we desire both the path and the gardens we have not yet seen.

The modern searcher for inner harmony embarks on a voyage—or several. Each voyage encourages self-observation and critical reflection. Each heightens awareness of the importance of specific aspects of our nature and becomes an indicator of exercise in those values. No two voyages are exactly the same, even though they may result in the same inner harmony. Each requires nurturing a particular set of aptitudes and sensibilities. The intellect, as one kind of faculty, appraises self-worth. But few voyages are as challenging as unburdening the score-keeping mind from fears, doubts, and resentments that had kept the self captive. In being freed from such negative influences, the self is transformed. We begin to see this new self as having won a game we had never thought of as a game, and that nobody had "won" until nothing praised or provoked.

We are socialized to get along with others, though we may think any implicit sense of differences is necessarily false. When others attack or unsettle us, we often retreat within ourselves and prioritize what we do not share with them. We play the game of standing back from situations. We fret over possible, yet improbable, psychic conflicts. We quarrel about principles. The more life away from the inner garden is lacking, the more we cherish it. We venerate the inner being yearned for and free of mainstream pollutants. Despite its apparent lack, we open ourselves into the managing calm. This invulnerability correlates significantly with the state of harmony.

CHAPTER 3

Section 2: Cultivating a Growth Mindset

To better comprehend the practices presented in the following sections, it is vital to understand the concept of a growth mindset. This section delves into what mindset is and provides ideas to guide readers in developing one. The fundamental truth is that we all carry within us limitless potential for personal and professional development. However, not everyone operates from that belief. Henry Ford's words articulate this divide perfectly: "Whether you think you can or think you can't, you're right." Those who believe they have the power and ability to change and grow in life generally succeed. Those who don't, generally don't. Consequently, the ideas discussed throughout this book are intended to help anyone shift towards a growth mindset.

What is Mindset?

Mindset is the established set of attitudes held by someone. Carol Dweck, a leading expert on mindset, posits that each of us has a mindset—a mental attitude that predetermines our interpretation of life experiences. These interpretations shape our behavior. A growth mindset is a mental attitude founded on the presupposition that you have the ability to develop, change, and grow. In contrast, a fixed mindset presupposes an incapability for growth and change. People can find themselves falling into either positive or negative mindsets in various aspects of their lives. The following sections provide a basis for cultivating growth or abundance mindsets. These practices are divided into four categories: emotional, mental, physical, and social, aiming to support personal development.

The Power of Beliefs and Mindsets

Overarching all other aspects of the **Soar to Success** framework are our beliefs and mindsets, the cornerstones of our thought life. They shape everything from our professional self-branding to our decision-making and approach to work. The beliefs and mindsets we hold can either impose limitations on our potential progress or enable us to break through these limitations. Consider your most long-held and deeply held beliefs, including those about yourself. What beliefs might hold you back, preventing you from reaching your true potential? Our beliefs tend to be self-perpetuating and self-referential. Once adopted, especially in our formative years, they reinforce each other. A belief about yourself, whether founded in fact or not, or an interpretation of an emotional state as 'stress' or a diagnosis of 'depression,' may be perpetuated and maintained over time. How do your beliefs affect your perceptions of others? How might they lead you to misjudge and misunderstand them?

Mindsets are a crucial part of our belief structure and drive our growth and evolution towards inner harmony. From a neuropsychological perspective, belief systems promote the release of serotonin, dopamine, and other 'happy' neurotransmitters, boosting confidence and resilience. Evidence suggests that when we find our primary purpose, supported by aligned anti-discriminatory, authenticity, and self-worth values, we can develop beliefs and strategies to live by these principles. Having a deep-seated, unshakable belief in your core self, living authentically, and aligning with your highest goals is what we call "Soaring to Success."

Overcoming Limiting Beliefs

The second practice for purpose is centered on shedding physical and psychological impediments that affect our ability to self-actualize. This involves enabling a fresh start: shedding weight can liberate us from a matrix that suffocates our dreams. We must also address physical impediments imposed by society that undermine our potential. Societal expectations can restrict teachers' capacities to transcend their roles and impose behaviors on leaders that limit their ability to grow.

Identifying limiting beliefs involves acknowledging which thoughts and aspirations are our own versus those imposed by others. External sources of limiting beliefs can include neglectful or overbearing parentage, controlling instruction, or dominance by authority figures. Social comparisons can be painful, from corporate competition to measuring our social worth by social media interactions. Social narratives at church, community, school, and workplace levels often reinforce limiting beliefs. Statements like "managerial folks in their mid-50s find the idea crazy" or societal expectations based on race, background, or education perpetuate these limitations. Career challenges may also be intertwined with legitimate hardships like income disparity and debt, which must be critiqued and addressed.

CHAPTER 4

Section 3: Setting Meaningful Goals

Our journey to soar to success begins with meaningful goal setting. Goals are the cornerstone of our success, igniting our passion, providing us with the willingness to do whatever it takes, and lighting the way for our evolution. To live a life without purpose, without worthy dreams or goals, is to drift aimlessly and react to the unexpected winds that blow. A worthy goal, clearly discussed and charted in our mind, gives us direction for our evolution.

There are two types of goals: outcome-based goals and practice-based goals. Most individuals are familiar with outcome-based goals. These are descriptive of what we want to achieve and inspire self-motivation by reminding us of our desired outcomes. Outcome-based goals provide the vision, while practice-based goals offer the roadmap. The willpower to act in our best interest often fades, but practice-based goals act as stepping-stones in the midst of this struggle.

Types of Goals

Some individuals might have a proclivity to set and achieve well-thought-out goals. They could possibly achieve all of them without needing to be constantly motivated, as these goals align deeply with their personal values. As success contains a large personal component, what one considers a success might not be seen as such by others. There are at least three types of goals that might be attained: subjective, fundamental, and subjective-fundamental goals.

- **Subjective Goals:** These are personal and unique to each individual. They are based on what one feels is important, regardless of societal expectations.
- **Fundamental Goals:** These align with cultural or societal values, such as money, power, prestige, and professional status.
- **Subjective-Fundamental Goals:** A blend of personal importance and societal values, where achieving these goals is crucial for the individual's self-worth and satisfaction.

Personal importance can be considered goal priorities, and there is no specific order in which goals can be achieved. The sufficiency or insufficiency of their attainment is a matter of subjective assessment. Goal attainment is a product of personal organizational action.

Goal-Setting Strategies

Idleness, indecision, and the lack of a clear path ahead can be sources of discomfort and suffering. This is how we drift if every step we take is involuntary and imposed by unforeseen circumstances. Even if we do not necessarily want to know what we will do a year from now or even tomorrow, these questions indicate personal purpose. They reflect an interest and a desire to lead our lives somewhere, beneficial whether you are an employee, a manager, or a student. In the end, if you are not paying the rent, someone else will decide what your life is supposed to be.

Setting meaningful goals involves several strategic steps:

1. **Identify Your Ideal Future:** Begin by envisioning your ideal time to come. Concentrate on your priorities and desires, not those of others.
2. **Write Down Your Goals:** Clearly articulate the results or achievements you want to accomplish. Writing them down solidifies your commitment.
3. **Break Down Goals into Manageable Steps:** Create smaller, actionable steps that lead to your larger goals. This makes the process less overwhelming and more achievable.
4. **Set Consistent and Feasible Daily Practices:** As Martha Beck, author of *The Four Day Win*, suggests, your goal should be to do one practice every day that is challenging enough to build willpower but manageable. For example, if you want to become a better service provider, set a goal of reading one chapter or article about your industry every workday.
5. **Consistency and Celebration:** The two Cs of goal setting are consistency and celebration. Make incremental progress daily, and celebrate even minor victories. Recognize and reward yourself for achieving daily goals to maintain motivation and momentum.

Vincent Lenhardt, a coach and philosopher, in his book *Know How to Say Yes to Yourself*, offers additional tips for those new to goal setting. His insights can help individuals in a dead end find their path forward.

CHAPTER 5

Section 4: Time Management and Productivity

Time management and productivity are integral to achieving success and maintaining a balanced, fulfilling life. This section explores effective strategies for managing your time and boosting productivity, transforming how you approach your daily tasks and long-term goals.

Understanding Time Management

Earlier, I mentioned my personal discovery about time management and how I've come to realize that the real goal isn't just to manage time but to manage life. Most people think it's about developing the right calendar or buying the right watch, but it's fundamentally about values, habits, and mental attitudes. Have you habitually banished the negative interruptions that drain your productivity, or do you surrender your attention to every latest thought? This lack of directed focus prevents purposeful momentum, leading to discontent and dissatisfaction. When our focus is directed and our interests clarified, a wave of contentment washes over us. Have you planned and then acted? Or has planning led to mere thinking and passive meditation instead of active advancement?

Effective Time Management Techniques

Time is an irreplaceable resource. Once lost, it cannot be recovered. Successful individuals manage their time differently, allowing them to accomplish more in the same amount of time. Effective time management involves:

- **Setting Clear Goals:** Clear goals give rise to creative and constructive ideas. Once goals are known, plans can be strategized effectively.
- **Prioritizing Tasks:** Schedule priorities first to ensure your week isn't filled with whatever comes across your desk. Set daily and weekly goals to introduce new ideas and people into your life.
- **Creating a Routine:** Allocate specific times for important activities. For example, spend 90 minutes in the morning and evening working on goals. Make appointments with yourself to develop new ideas and meet new people each day.
- **Delegating Tasks:** Learn to delegate tasks that others can do better, freeing up time for more critical activities.

Boosting Productivity

Productivity is not just about working harder but working smarter. Here are ten practices to find success through purpose, inner harmony, and growth:

1. **Self-Care:** Go back to the fundamentals of self-care to boost productivity and find your sense of purpose. Healthline offers strategies for those in the gig economy, emphasizing the importance of self-management.
2. **Be Aggressively Good to Yourself:** Adopt practices that promote self-compassion and resilience.

3. **Address Burnout:** Recognize and address burnout to maintain productivity. Leah Weiss, PhD, highlights the importance of addressing burnout to achieve long-term success.
4. **TILT (Draw Inwards):** Use the Horizon Work symbol of TILT to draw inward and focus on personal growth and healing. Writing down thoughts in a journal can track progress and changes.
5. **Meditation and Yoga:** Incorporate meditation and yoga into your routine for mental and physical well-being.
6. **Time Blocking:** Allocate specific time blocks for tasks to ensure focused work sessions.
7. **Limit Distractions:** Identify and eliminate distractions that impede productivity.
8. **Break Tasks into Manageable Steps:** Divide larger tasks into smaller, actionable steps to make them more manageable.
9. **Regularly Review Goals:** Take time to review and adjust goals to stay aligned with your long-term vision.
10. **Celebrate Achievements:** Recognize and celebrate even minor achievements to maintain motivation and momentum.

CHAPTER 6

Section 5: Building Resilience and Overcoming Chal

Embarking on the journey to success requires mindful choices and readiness to take action. Opportunities are intertwined with the challenges each person faces. How can one become more purpose-driven, embracing beauty and consciousness? This section provides techniques to navigate challenges with integrity, congruency, and alignment, helping you stay resilient as obstacles arise.

Understanding Resilience

Resilience is the strength we must add to our toolkit as we walk the path toward success. It refers to our ability to cope with and overcome adversity. Adversity comes in many forms, from death and illness to financial problems and personal inadequacies. Some adversities are catastrophic, while others are mundane. Resilience helps us rise above adversity by equipping us with the tools to confront and conquer it.

As you read this book, you will learn about the failures that occasionally rear their unwelcome heads on the path to success. Resilience allows you to confront these barriers without undue disillusionment. For some, the goal may be great treasure; for others, it might be successfully raising a family, becoming a strong and resilient leader, or achieving inner harmony. At a minimum, we hope to make it through life with our sanity, health, emotions, and self-worth intact.

Resilience is an absolute necessity. Succeeding in whatever life throws at us demands perseverance and adaptability. Aqua-colored water cannot be anything other than aqua-colored water; its makeup remains unchanged. In the same way, resilience is inherent in our character.

Strategies for Overcoming Challenges

Staying the course when things aren't working can be tough. Knowing what strategies to use can help you stay on track rather than abandoning your efforts and vision. Here are some strategies to consider when facing daily pressures and setbacks:

1. **Visualize Success:** Imagine a carefree and successful future. This focus can create a mental vacuum that nature abhors, filling it with positive possibilities. Not being able to articulate a vision might indicate a lack of inspiration or a restricted point of view. Focusing on what is truly important shifts your energy and attention to possibilities instead of limitations.
2. **Develop a Positive Mindset:** Embrace a growth mindset, believing in your ability to develop and grow. This mindset helps you view challenges as opportunities for growth rather than insurmountable obstacles.
3. **Set Realistic Goals:** Break down your goals into manageable steps. This makes the process less overwhelming and more achievable, allowing you to celebrate small victories along the way.

4. **Practice Self-Care:** Taking care of your physical, emotional, and mental well-being is crucial. Engage in activities that replenish your energy and maintain a healthy balance.
5. **Build a Support Network:** Surround yourself with supportive individuals who encourage and motivate you. Sharing your struggles and successes with others can provide valuable insights and boost your resilience.
6. **Learn from Failures:** View failures as learning experiences rather than setbacks. Each failure provides an opportunity to grow and improve, bringing you one step closer to success.
7. **Stay Flexible:** Adaptability is key to overcoming challenges. Be open to changing your approach and trying new strategies when faced with obstacles.
8. **Maintain Focus:** Avoid distractions and stay focused on your goals. Prioritize tasks that align with your long-term vision and dedicate time to working on them consistently.

By incorporating these strategies into your daily life, you can build resilience and overcome challenges, paving the way for success and inner harmony.

CHAPTER 7

Section 6: Nurturing Inner Harmony

While purpose is the main driver of success, inner harmony is the platform from which that success launches. Neurological science shows that your brain's capacities for higher thought are significantly enhanced if you are healthy physically and emotionally. Achieving this starts with a reasonably healthy diet, regular exercise, adequate sleep, and sufficient hydration. Purposeful success that is solid and lasting also revolves around daily practice.

Freedom from Imbalance

Creating daily practices to maintain emotional balance is essential. One timeless technique is deep breathing, which has long been recognized for its merits. Practicing deep breathing regularly in a calm, peaceful setting can clear a busy mind and release pent-up emotions. Tai Chi, an ancient Chinese martial art, is also highly effective for emotional balance. Practitioners report that emotions like anger, fear, and worry dissipate through regular practice. Both exercises must be practiced consistently to be completely effective, but they show obvious results in just a few minutes.

Connecting with Nature

Getting outdoors and connecting with nature is another powerful way to nurture inner harmony. If you regularly engage in outdoor activities, you are already experiencing internal harmonization. If not, find ways to connect with nature daily. Ask yourself: "What small action can I take to be in a natural environment every day?" The natural world provides sensory input that leads to experiences beyond your busy mind, taking you out of internal questions and focusing on the multi-sensory setting around you. The sound of the wind, the warmth of the sun, and twigs cracking underfoot are unique experiences that cannot be processed in abstract thought. This focus on nature opens up mental space, making conscious awareness suddenly possible.

Mindfulness Practices

Mindfulness practices help bring you back to your center, especially good to start the day. These practices build present-moment awareness, supporting focus and preventing distractions. Daily repetition of these ideas—five minutes at a time—promotes inner harmony and peacefulness.

- **Morning Practice:** Spend five minutes lying in bed, mentally considering that you are "awake in peace and not disturbed."
- **Day Review:** As you review your day, do so with your "eyes closed," imagining that the scenario has not yet come true. You are at peace and wake up as planned and on time.
- **Evening Practice:** Before you sleep, spend five minutes slowing down your thoughts, considering that sleep is coming: "I go to bed in peace—peacefully and on time." Empty your mind of worries and fears so the messages to your control center are constructive ones.

Self-Compassion and Self-Care

Self-Compassion

According to Kristin Neff, self-compassion includes three components:

1. **Self-Kindness:** It's critical to care for yourself.
2. **Common Humanity:** Recognize that everyone is interconnected in the human experience, which is an effective method to combat loneliness in times of crisis.
3. **Mindfulness of Imperfection:** Understand and accept that everyone makes mistakes. Realize that failure is common and temporary, offering yourself the same compassion you would to a friend who is struggling.

Self-Care

Soar to Success' three principles of inner harmony are interconnected. When we trust ourselves with self-compassion and a peaceful purpose, it becomes simpler to make time for self-nurturing. Mindful attention to the needs of mind, body, and career allows for adequate rest and renewal.

- **Morning Ritual:** If you prepare juice for your kids before they go to school, juice a little extra for yourself. Sip and enjoy it while greeting the morning, taking a few moments to look at the sunrise outdoors. If you don't juice, opt for hot chocolate or herbal tea. Regardless of the drink, savor the moment and your surroundings.

By incorporating these practices into your daily routine, you can nurture inner harmony, paving the way for a balanced and successful life.

CHAPTER 8

Section 7: Cultivating Positive Relationships

Personal growth and success flourish when we feel supported. Building strong, meaningful connections with others is essential. Empathy is the glue that fosters deep connections, but it requires effort and vulnerability. Learning to manage conflict effectively can also transform challenges into opportunities for growth.

Building Empathy and Connection

Empathy is more than just feeling for a person; it is feeling with them, which deepens connection. Empathic connection is crucial for relationships across various contexts, including client-therapist, student-educator, and co-worker relationships. Empathy requires tuning into another person, becoming vulnerable ourselves, and allowing the process of healing to take place. This can be challenging because we often seek quick fixes to silence pain rather than letting it emerge.

Research highlights several ways to build empathy:

1. **Mindfulness Practice:** Meditation strengthens the brain's mirror neurons and prefrontal cortex, enhancing our ability

to empathize and take other people's perspectives. Yoga also fosters bodily empathy, helping us attune to posture, movement, and gesture.
2. **Becoming a Better Listener:** Truly listening to others without interrupting or offering unsolicited advice shows that you value their experiences and emotions.
3. **Random Acts of Kindness:** Small, thoughtful actions can create a ripple effect, enhancing empathy and connection.

Empathy is a skill that can be cultivated through practice and intention. By making an effort to understand and share the feelings of others, we can build stronger, more meaningful relationships.

Conflict Resolution Skills

Conflict is inevitable, but it can be an opportunity for growth if managed well. Effective conflict resolution involves:

1. **Active Listening:** Clearly restate opponents' views with your own additions, ensuring you understand their perspective.
2. **Agree and Concede:** Find common ground by agreeing or conceding points when appropriate. This shows respect and willingness to collaborate.
3. **Adding Your Perspective:** Share your thoughts and interpretations in a way that contributes to the conversation constructively, using humor if appropriate.
4. **Reciprocity:** Ensure that both parties have an opportunity to speak and listen, fostering mutual respect and understanding.

These skills help maintain presence during conflicts, allowing for constructive dialogue and collaborative solutions. Practicing these techniques can strengthen relationships and enhance overall communication.

Social Connections and Well-being

Positive social connections increase life expectancy, boost immune response, and can be an antidote to depression. Building and maintaining these connections requires effort, but the benefits are profound. Here are some strategies to enhance your social connections:

- **Reach Out:** Make an effort to connect with others regularly, whether through social events, group activities, or one-on-one interactions.
- **Show Empathy:** Demonstrate that you "get" what others are feeling by acknowledging their emotions and showing understanding.
- **Be Present:** Stay fully engaged in conversations, avoiding distractions like smartphones or multitasking.
- **Resolve Conflicts:** Use effective conflict resolution skills to address and resolve issues promptly, preventing misunderstandings and strengthening relationships.

By cultivating empathy, practicing effective conflict resolution, and building positive social connections, you can enhance your personal growth and success.

CHAPTER 9

Section 8: Embracing Change and Adaptability

One of the clichés often heard from leadership coaches, writers, and speakers is "The only constant is change." While it may sound trite, it holds a profound truth. Change is a constant, and continual change—on a massive scale—defines the era in which we live. Living with purpose in this context requires flexibility, adaptability, and resilience.

The Nature of Change

Change is an undeniable part of life. We encounter it everywhere, even if we resist it. Assessments of career paths, industries, businesses, or specific departments predict that many of the jobs today's young people will hold in the future haven't even been created yet! Beyond the job market, change is pervasive: cultural, social, political, economic, and environmental turbulence have become the norm. As we anticipate continual change as surely as the sun sets and rises, we must embrace the idea that change can make us stronger and enrich our lives.

Despite the turbulence, we have adapted. The 2012 presentation of the World Happiness Report noted, "The 'happiness' levels of the people in a country can rise or fall in response to changes in the natural environment, whether it's economic booms or busts, or changes in government." Joblessness, divorce, and natural disasters can shake the core of our "happiness," but generally, we are more adaptable than we sometimes realize. We are in charge of our adaptability in this era of uncertainties.

The natural approach to SOAR (Strengths, Opportunities, Aspirations, Results) practice can inform organizational life, helping to think about and execute change in new and effective ways. It provides insights that traditional planning methods may lack, offering a perspective on how organizations and careers should structure themselves to grow into the future. Everyday processes, simple meetings, and complete strategic plans based on the organic world help us see the next steps through a lens focused on "what is better."

Walking the Woods

For those who enjoy spending time in the woods, consider the view from four decades ago that suggested cleaning the woods by clear-cutting. Today, we understand that downed trees provide nutrients to growing trees. Nutrients pass from tree to tree through fungi, which distribute nutrients evenly across the forest floor. Clearing debris can disrupt this natural flow of resources, harming emerging forests. This analogy illustrates the importance of allowing natural processes to guide us through change.

Adapting to Change

Navigating change, whether forced or chosen, involves potential risks. Initial discomfort or fear of the unknown is common, but with time, we adapt to new situations. Research by Mills and Kellogg found that individuals who were laid off initially experienced psychological stress, but the effects dissipated within six months. Physically healthy people are mentally adaptable, and with practice, we can cultivate both physical and mental adaptability.

The ability to adapt can be enhanced through physical, mental, and emotional practice:

- **Physical Activities:** Martial arts, dance, or other physical activities help develop the skills necessary to meet new physical requirements. These activities integrate the body's natural cycles with the rhythms of our ever-changing environment, creating seamless adaptation to new demands.
- **Mental Flexibility:** Improvisation in theatre and dance, being present in the moment, and simple awareness training can cultivate mental adaptability. These practices help us stay attuned to the real world from moment to moment, enhancing our resilience.
- **Emotional Resilience:** Developing emotional resilience involves acknowledging and processing our emotions rather than suppressing them. Mindfulness and meditation practices can strengthen our emotional adaptability, helping us navigate unpredictable surprises.

By embracing change and cultivating adaptability, we can thrive in the face of uncertainty and transform challenges into opportunities for growth.

CHAPTER 10

Conclusion

This book is intended to offer vantage points and best practices in purpose and inner harmony. The "Soar to Success Path" provides inspiring questions, provocative insights, wise proverbs, compelling stories, and voices of experience. Most importantly, it offers immediate and long-term application tools. To make a significant difference in your professional and personal lives, you will need to read, re-read, journal, apply, and reflect on the concepts to sew lasting wisdom into your thought patterns and actions.

We conclude with the main message of this book in the form of verities and certainties, steps, principles, theories, paradoxes, and disciplines for action. There is a habitual, instantaneous term all of us must promise: "The Fruitfulness of Confluence is Integrity." What others term a habitual personality of endeavors for increased effectiveness and efficiency, we see as the most powerful view of achieving purposeful success in personal and professional life. Managing a life for inner harmony becomes the foundation of innovative solutions and targeted outcomes.

The triumph in your personal life and success at work are meant for your flourishing. These transformative movements concentrate on manifesting, applying, and achieving the results we predict. We discuss grounds for strong, internal, positively charged traditional fitness for purpose participants. To catalyze results toward purpose and inner harmony, we offer hope for unifying forces such as gaining insight into oneself through personality tests and spiritual quotient; boosting mental wellness through neuro-linguistic programming and perceptual thinking; and strengthening cognitive fitness for understanding others through teaching emotional competence.

As these talents form the core of any purposeful, restorative, and confluence management, our book's action barriers allow you to dig in, hike gently on the path, become a leader of top efficiency, and exploit the full payoffs of consequence. As champions of your supreme success, we hope you reap the heightened contact and inner harmony in your life!

Key Takeaways and Action Steps
Now what?

If you are interested in integrating these practices into your life, here are some approaches:

- **Weekly Reading and Reflection:** Each week, read the narrative at the beginning, try the practices for a few days, and give yourself time for reflection at the end of the week. Begin the new week with the next narrative.
- **Structured Approach:** Hold off on reading the reflection questions until you've engaged in the practices a few times. Then, have a lengthy meditation or writing session. Alternatively, use the reflection questions consistently but for shorter periods.
- **Creating a Personal Roadmap:** Create a personal and authentic roadmap, tested over time, providing the scientific underpinning for many spiritual and psychotherapeutic practices. This book organizes the roadmap into three insights:

1. **Psychological and Spiritual Growth:** Engage in practices fostering psychological and spiritual growth.
2. **Sense of a Life Well-Lived:** These practices contribute to a hearty life.
3. **Cultural Paradigms:** A hearty life fosters success in central cultural paradigms, such as at work, in school, or at home.

By following these steps and integrating these insights, you can create a roadmap that supports your journey toward purpose and inner harmony.

Milton Keynes UK
Ingram Content Group UK Ltd.
UKHW040054031224
451863UK00004B/274